IN THE RAIN

I believe in

fabulous

flamingos

Christina Rose

I believe in fabulous flamingos
a funky flamingo colouring book

ISBN: 978-1-912155-62-0

Created by Christina Rose

Contributors: Letitia Clouden, Shutterstock

www.bellmackenzie.com

BELL & MACKENZIE
PUBLISHING LIMITED

I believe in fabulous flamingos

I believe in fabulous flamingos

I believe in fabulous flamingos

I believe in fabulous flamingos

I believe in fabulous flamingos

I believe in fabulous flamingos

I believe in fabulous flamingos

I believe in fabulous flamingos

I believe in fabulous flamingos

I believe in fabulous flamingos

I believe in fabulous flamingos

I believe in fabulous flamingos

I believe in fabulous flamingos

I believe in fabulous flamingos

I believe in fabulous flamingos

I believe in fabulous flamingos

I believe in fabulous flamingos

I believe in fabulous flamingos

I believe in fabulous flamingos

I believe in fabulous flamingos

I believe in fabulous flamingos

I believe in fabulous flamingos

I believe in fabulous flamingos

I believe in fabulous flamingos

I believe in fabulous flamingos

I believe in fabulous flamingos

I believe in fabulous flamingos

I believe in fabulous flamingos

I believe in fabulous flamingos

I believe in fabulous flamingos

I believe in fabulous flamingos

I believe in fabulous flamingos

I believe in fabulous flamingos

I believe in fabulous flamingos

I believe in fabulous flamingos

I believe in fabulous flamingos

I believe in fabulous flamingos

I believe in fabulous flamingos

I believe in fabulous flamingos

I believe in fabulous flamingos

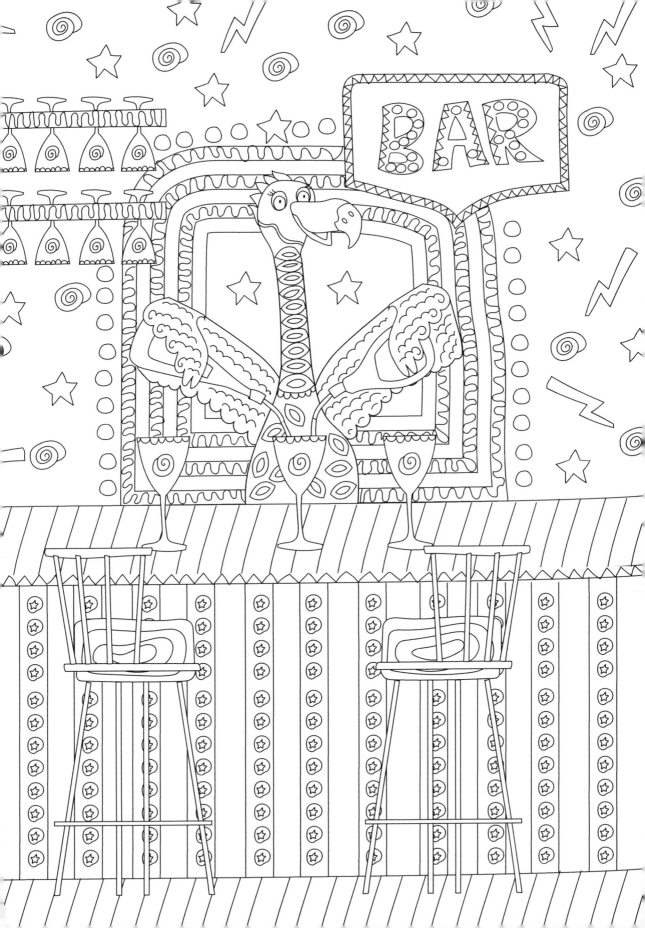

I believe in fabulous flamingos

I believe in fabulous flamingos

I believe in fabulous flamingos

I believe in fabulous flamingos

I believe in fabulous flamingos

I believe in fabulous flamingos

Made in the USA
Columbia, SC
25 February 2021